# THE VANISHED
# NORTHWEST PASSAGE
# ARCTIC EXPEDITION

by Lisa M. Bolt Simons • illustrated by Eugene Smith

CAPSTONE PRESS
a capstone imprint

Graphic Library is published by Capstone Press, an imprint of Capstone.
1710 Roe Crest Drive
North Mankato, Minnesota 56003
capstonepub.com

Library of Congress Cataloging-in-Publication Data
Names: Simons, Lisa M. B., 1969- author. | Smith, Eugene (Illustrator), illustrator.
Title: The vanished Northwest Passage Arctic expedition / by Lisa M. Bolt Simons ;
illustrated by Eugene Smith.
Description: North Mankato, Minnesota : Capstone Press, 2022. | Series: Deadly
expeditions | Includes bibliographical references and index. | Audience: Ages
8-11 | Audience: Grades 4-6 | Summary: "In 1845, Sir John Franklin commanded
two ships on an expedition to find a Northwest Passage from England through
the Arctic and over to Asia. If successful, the route would be a faster way to get
goods from Asia to Europe and back. But success was not in the cards for Franklin's
expedition. Only recently, the sunken ships were discovered in the icy Arctic
waters. What happened to Franklin and his men, and what messages did they leave
behind?"— Provided by publisher.
Identifiers: LCCN 2021029801 (print) | LCCN 2021029802 (ebook) | ISBN
9781663958921 (hardcover) | ISBN 9781666322446 (paperback) | ISBN
9781666322453 (pdf) | ISBN 9781666322477 (kindle edition)
Subjects: LCSH: John Franklin Arctic Expedition (1845-1851)—Juvenile literature.
| Northwest Passage—Discovery and exploration—British—Juvenile literature.
| Franklin, John, 1786-1847—Juvenile literature. | Explorers—Great Britain—
Biography—Juvenile literature.
Classification: LCC G660 .S56 2022 (print) | LCC G660 (ebook) | DDC
910.9163/27—dc23
LC record available at https://lccn.loc.gov/2021029801
LC ebook record available at https://lccn.loc.gov/2021029802

Editorial Credits
Editor: Mandy Robbins; Designer: Dina Her; Media Researcher: Jo Miller;
Production Specialist: Tori Abraham

All internet sites appearing in back matter were available and accurate when this
book was sent to press.

Printed and bound in the USA. PO4608

# TABLE OF CONTENTS

1845. London, England. Sir John Franklin and his wife, Lady Jane Franklin, had just returned from Van Diemen's Land, now called Tasmania. Franklin had been lieutenant-governor there from 1837 to 1843.

I cannot believe I'll soon be 60 years old.

Indeed! Shall we celebrate?

What is there to celebrate? Van Diemen's Land was a disaster. I tried to help the people, but they resented the government.

So many lies were spread about me. I must regain my reputation!

What if you led another expedition to the Arctic?

Franklin had served in the British Navy since the age of 14. He had been part of three famous—or infamous—Arctic journeys. In 1818, he had sailed on the *Trent* as second-in-command. They tried to reach the North Pole but didn't make it.

Franklin also led a journey from the Hudson Bay to the Arctic Ocean. This expedition helped Franklin map North America's unexplored Arctic coast. He and his crew were gone from 1819 to 1822.

It had been an agonizing journey. The ships got stuck in the ice. They ran out of food. Ten men died. Desperate, Franklin ate his shoe leather before the crew was rescued. He became known throughout the British Empire as "The Man Who Ate His Boots."

From 1824 to 1828, Captain Franklin led another expedition. It added 1,200 miles (1,931 kilometers) of shoreline to the maps of what the English knew about the Arctic geography. But there was still one Arctic adventure Franklin longed for.

Narrative of a Second Expedition to the Shores of THE POLAR SEA, in the Years 1825, 1826, and 1827

BY JOHN FRANKLIN

If you can find a water route through North America, you'll restore your good name.

You're right, and I must do it before anyone else does!

Do you remember those ships we saw in Van Diemen's?

Yes—with Ross and Crozier!

In 1809, Francis Crozier had left Ireland to join the Royal Navy at the age of 13.

Crozier quickly showed his worth among the Navy officials. He joined several expeditions. He met officer James Clark Ross in 1821 on an Arctic expedition, and they became friends. Crozier also made friends with the Inuit people who lived there and learned their language.

Crozier served as lieutenant on ships for more than 20 years. In 1839, Ross asked him to command the HMS *Terror*. Ross took command of the HMS *Erebus*. The first expedition for the *Erebus* and the *Terror* headed to Antarctica.

In August 1840, Ross and Crozier met Franklin while he was serving as lieutenant-governor of Van Diemen's Land.

What fine ships, Captain Ross.

Yes, they were built to withstand bombs . . .

Of course.

. . . but they've been refitted to push through ice.

You could use them to find the Northwest Passage, John!

They would be perfect.

Finding the Northwest Passage would be wonderful for trade!

In 1845, Franklin finally got his chance to command an Arctic exploration to find the Northwest Passage. Crozier captained the *Terror* and was Franklin's second-in-command. Franklin captained the *Erebus*. A man named James Fitzjames was the commanding officer under Franklin. Unfortunately, Fitzjames chose inexperienced crewmen for the expedition.

Only two other men have Arctic experience aside from Captain Franklin and me.

Out of a crew of 134? It's quite odd. And Franklin hasn't commanded a ship through the ice since when?

Many years. I fear we will blunder in the ice.

Had I not promised my wife to give up Arctic exploration, I would go with you. Good luck, my friend.

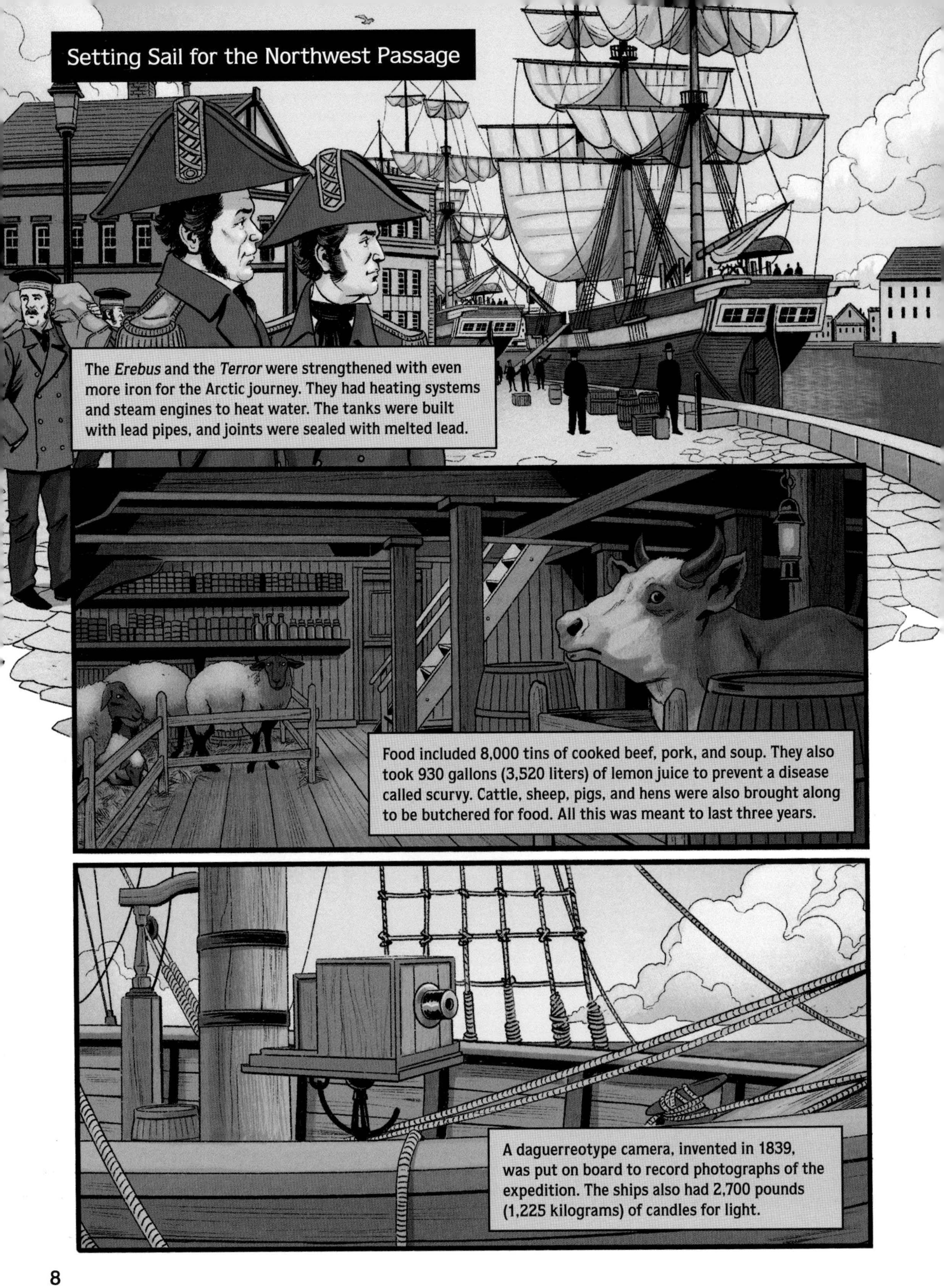
Setting Sail for the Northwest Passage
The *Erebus* and the *Terror* were strengthened with even more iron for the Arctic journey. They had heating systems and steam engines to heat water. The tanks were built with lead pipes, and joints were sealed with melted lead.
Food included 8,000 tins of cooked beef, pork, and soup. They also took 930 gallons (3,520 liters) of lemon juice to prevent a disease called scurvy. Cattle, sheep, pigs, and hens were also brought along to be butchered for food. All this was meant to last three years.
A daguerreotype camera, invented in 1839, was put on board to record photographs of the expedition. The ships also had 2,700 pounds (1,225 kilograms) of candles for light.

I see they're loading the *Erebus* with some animals. Friends of yours, Sir?

My wife wanted me to take the dog as a companion. The cat can eat rats, and the monkey can entertain the men.

Finally, the ships were ready for the crew to board.

At least Fitzjames found a crew that is young and strong.

Even if inexperienced in the Arctic.

On May 19, 1845, the crew and officers said goodbye to their families. The ships left Greenhithe, England, on the River Thames and headed out into the North Sea. They sailed around Scotland and headed west to cross the Atlantic Ocean.

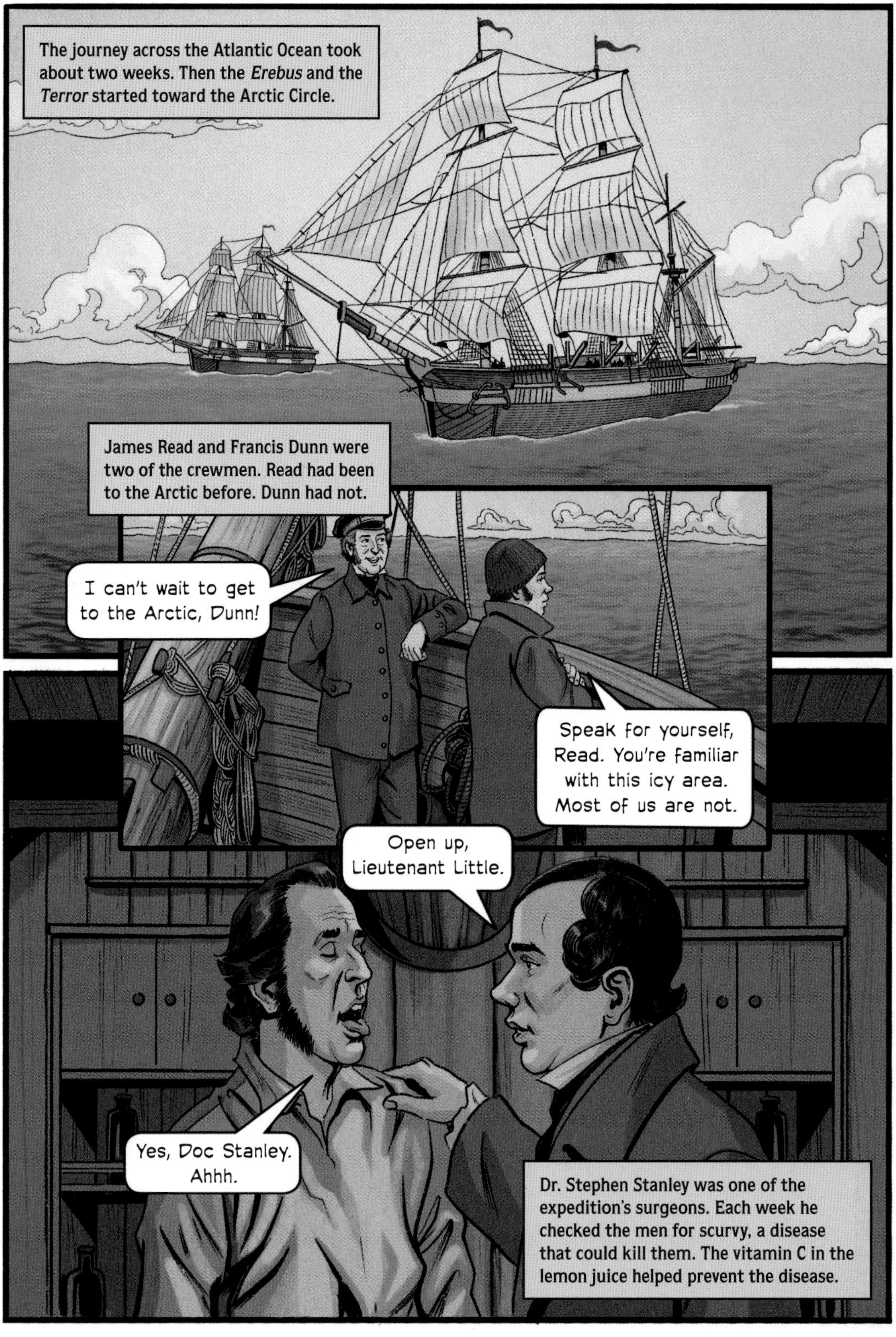
The journey across the Atlantic Ocean took about two weeks. Then the *Erebus* and the *Terror* started toward the Arctic Circle.
James Read and Francis Dunn were two of the crewmen. Read had been to the Arctic before. Dunn had not.
I can't wait to get to the Arctic, Dunn!
Speak for yourself, Read. You're familiar with this icy area. Most of us are not.
Open up, Lieutenant Little.
Yes, Doc Stanley. Ahhh.
Dr. Stephen Stanley was one of the expedition's surgeons. Each week he checked the men for scurvy, a disease that could kill them. The vitamin C in the lemon juice helped prevent the disease.

In July 1845, two months after leaving England, the *Erebus* and the *Terror* stopped at the Whale Fish Islands off the coast of Greenland. There, the crew loaded more supplies onto the ships. The men wrote their last letters home. Five sick men returned to London on the supply ships. They had no idea how lucky they were.

*James I wish you were here, I would then have no doubt as to our pursuing the proper course . . .*

*Yours most sincerely,*
*FRM Crozier*

The ships could only stay a matter of days. They wanted to beat the ice.

As you've seen, the water contains more ice.

Prepare your clothing and provisions. We leave for the Arctic tomorrow morning.

The air will only grow colder.

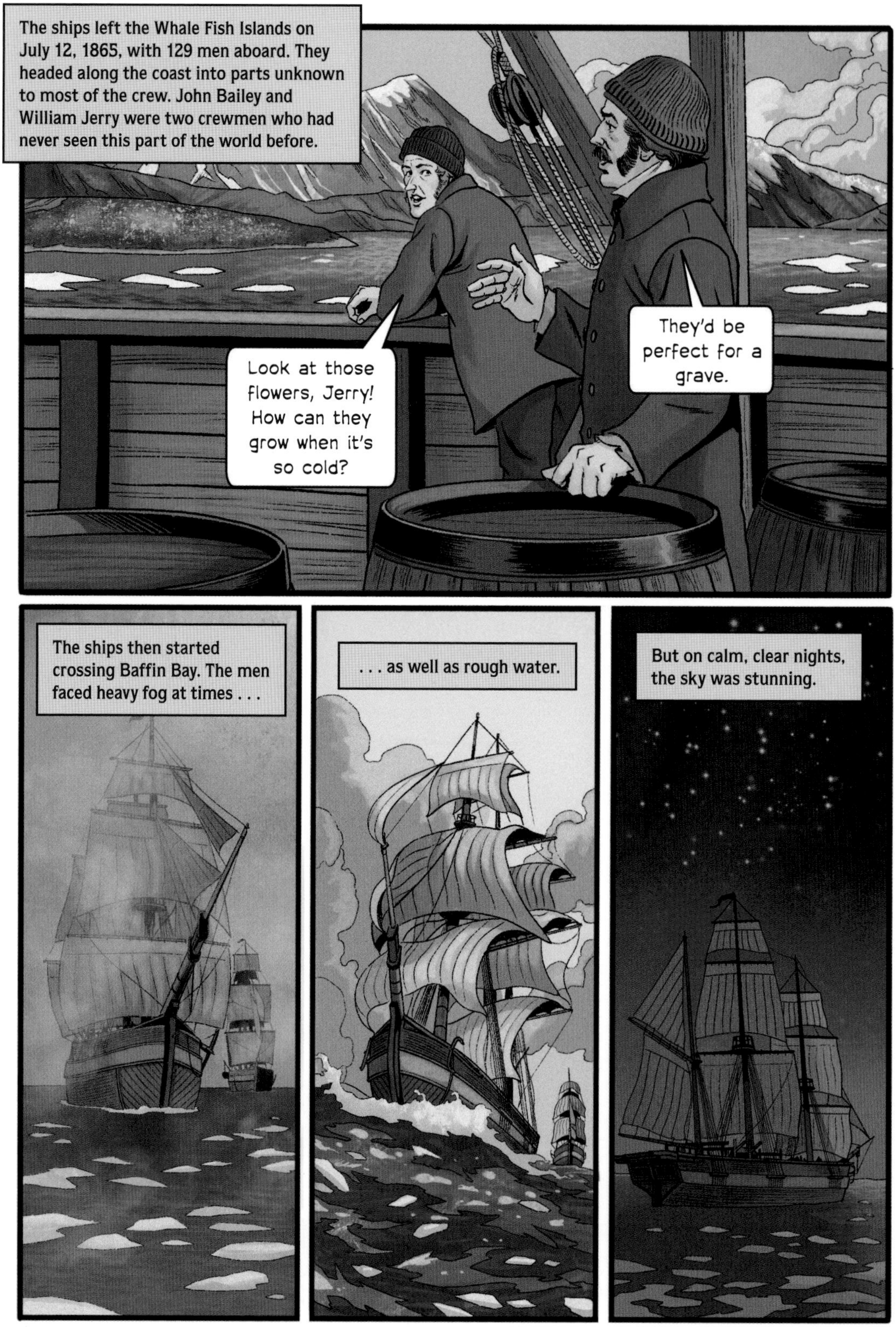
The ships left the Whale Fish Islands on July 12, 1865, with 129 men aboard. They headed along the coast into parts unknown to most of the crew. John Bailey and William Jerry were two crewmen who had never seen this part of the world before.
Look at those flowers, Jerry! How can they grow when it's so cold?
They'd be perfect for a grave.
The ships then started crossing Baffin Bay. The men faced heavy fog at times . . .
. . . as well as rough water.
But on calm, clear nights, the sky was stunning.

Expeditions included making observations of the wildlife. Narwhals, also called sea unicorns, lived around Greenland.

Look, Captain Crozier! Sea unicorns!

Indeed, Bailey. Please note in the logbook, Lieutenant Little.

How long must we wait, Captain?

Until we can break through this ice, Fitzjames.

A couple of weeks had passed. But the ships couldn't leave Baffin Bay because there was too much ice in present-day Lancaster Sound.

Near the end of July 1845, the crew of a whaling ship in Baffin Bay saw the *Erebus* and the *Terror* as they waited to enter Lancaster Sound. This is the last time these ships were seen afloat by Europeans.

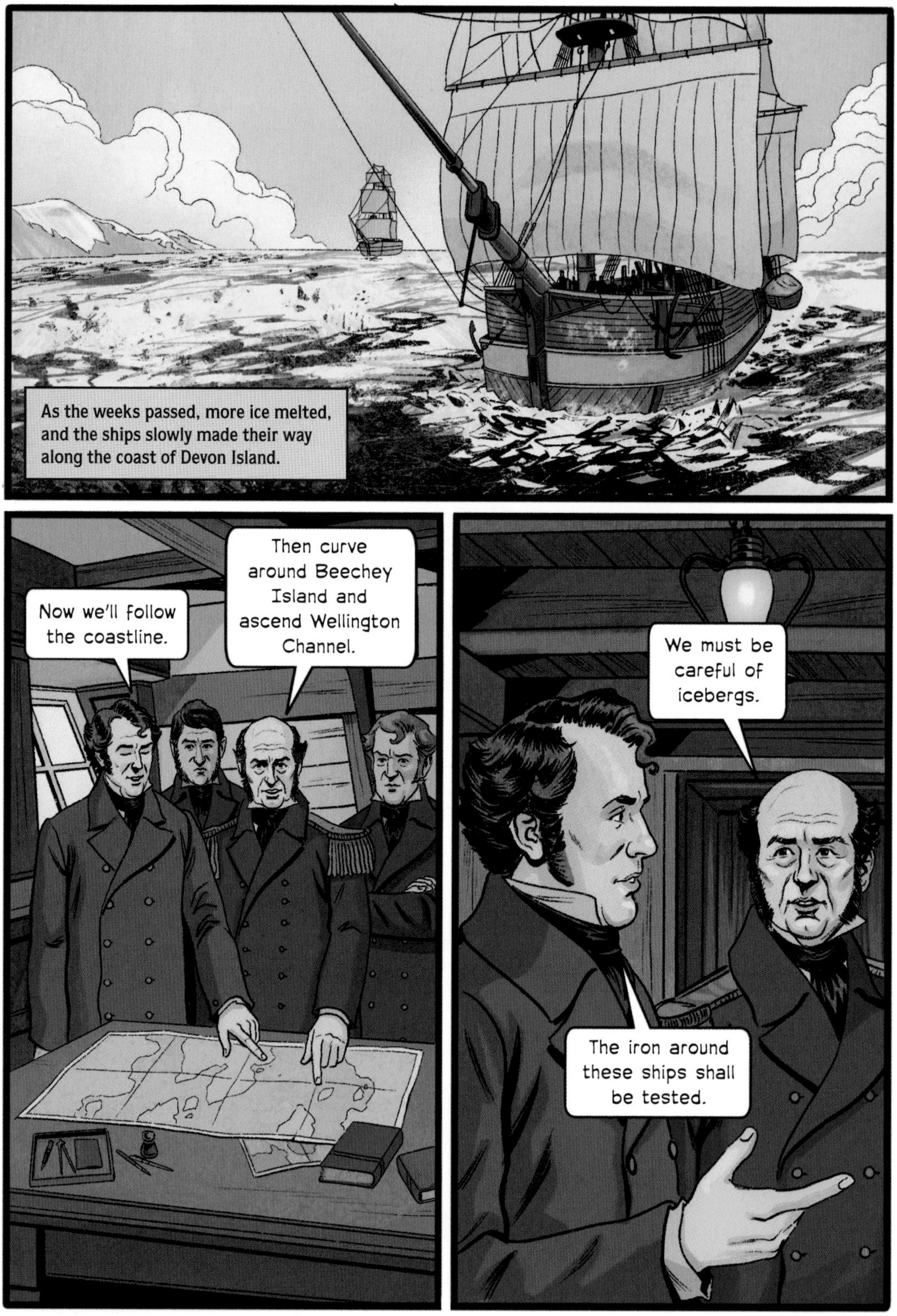
As the weeks passed, more ice melted, and the ships slowly made their way along the coast of Devon Island.
Now we'll follow the coastline.
Then curve around Beechey Island and ascend Wellington Channel.
We must be careful of icebergs.
The iron around these ships shall be tested.

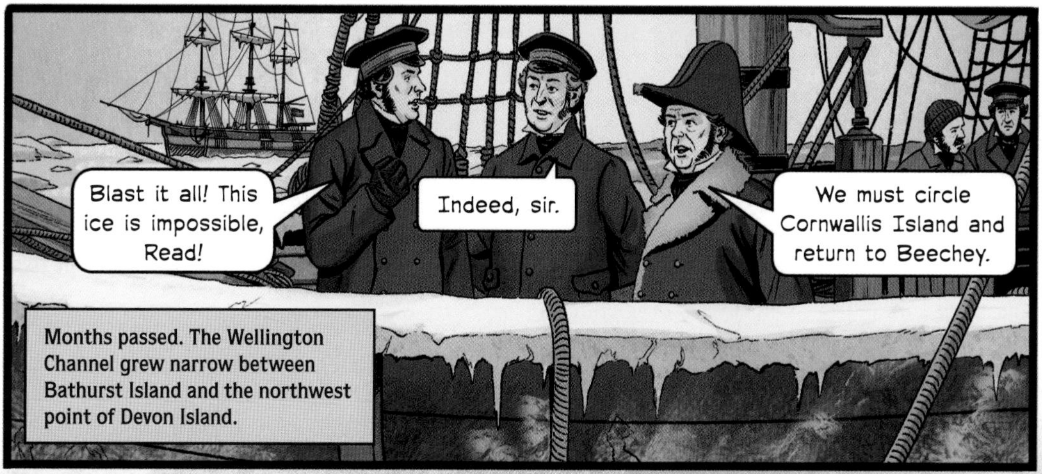
Blast it all! This ice is impossible, Read!
Indeed, sir.
We must circle Cornwallis Island and return to Beechey.
Months passed. The Wellington Channel grew narrow between Bathurst Island and the northwest point of Devon Island.

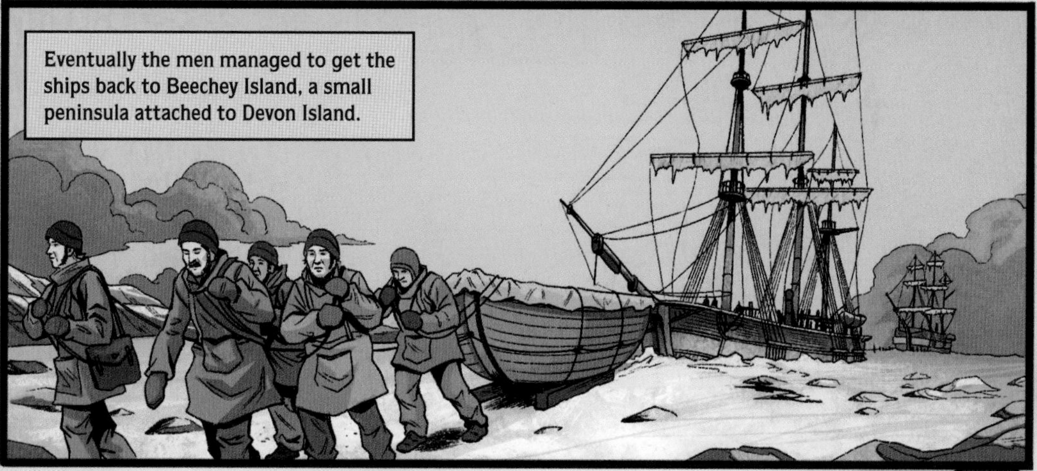
Eventually the men managed to get the ships back to Beechey Island, a small peninsula attached to Devon Island.

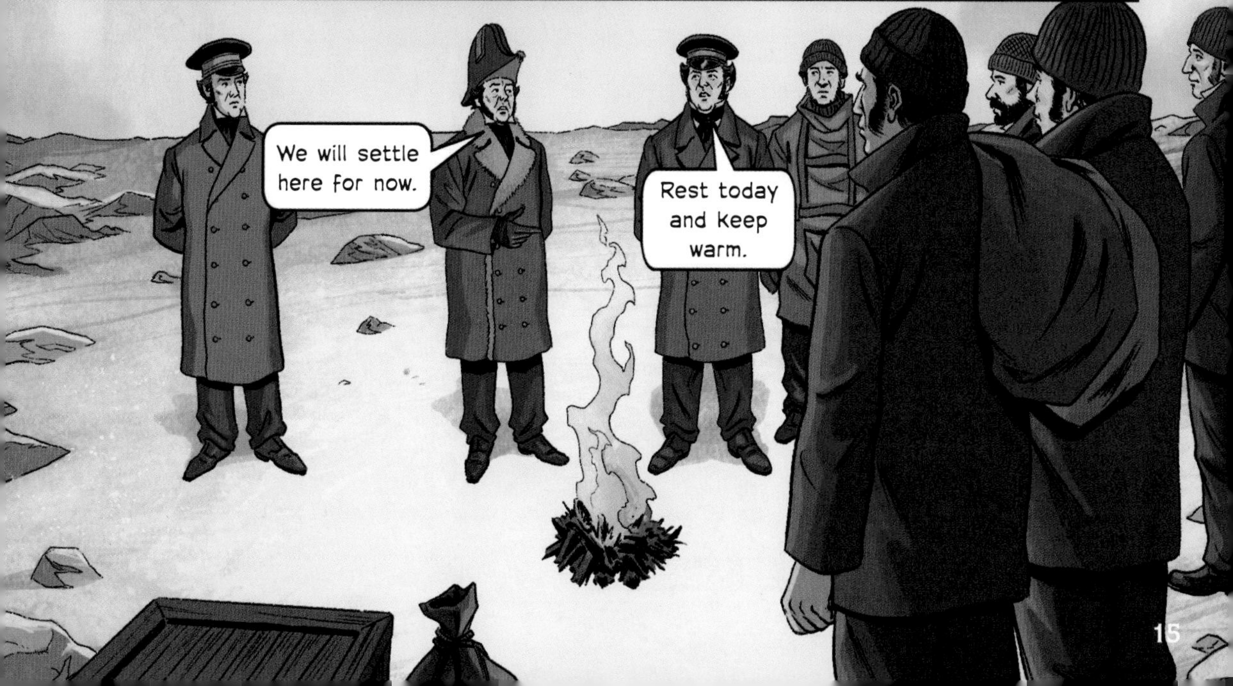
We will settle here for now.
Rest today and keep warm.

In the autumn of 1845, the *Erebus* and the *Terror* crews settled in to spend the winter on Beechey Island. Temperatures during the day were minus 31 degrees Fahrenheit (minus 35 degrees Celsius) and dropped to -54°F (-48°C) during the night.

Braine, Cann, Hartnell, and Torrington! You're on exploration today.

During the days, the officers sent out crewmen to explore the island.

What a beast he is, Braine!

Certainly, Hartnell. Unlike us, he loves this horrible cold!

I took off my cap too fast, Dr. Peddie.

Oh, Mr. Cann! The sealskin froze to your skin and ripped it off your forehead.

Besides frostbite, the extreme cold sometimes did other damage to a crewman's body. Dr. Peddie, the ship's doctor on the *Terror*, often treated them.

At night, the crew entertained themselves with barrel organs, writing, and reading. The ship libraries had almost 3,000 books and magazines.

COUGH COUGH COUGH

My sweat turned to ice after pushing that sledge.

You should've changed into dry underwear.

Shoveling coal into the firebox had me sweating too.

For some crewmen, the extreme cold made them very sick.

May they rest in peace.

On January 1, 1846, 20-year-old John Torrington died. Three days later, 25-year-old Josh Hartnell died.

Just imagine the riches, gentlemen.

After Torrington and Hartnell died, it was hard to keep the men's spirits up. Ice Masters Read and Blanky continued to speak of the wonders of the Arctic. Captains Franklin and Crozier spoke of the Northwest Passage and how its control would benefit Britain.

The beauty of the northern nights also gave the men a spectacular sight to see many nights.

What are those beautiful dancing lights?

The northern lights, Coombs, also called aurora borealis. They're lovely, aren't they?

Some men still struggled with the bitter cold.

The frostbite was too bad, Commander.

A rotting disease called gangrene set in.

How bad?

I had to cut off four toes on one foot and three on the other.

How is Officer Reddington now?

Better. Resting.

18

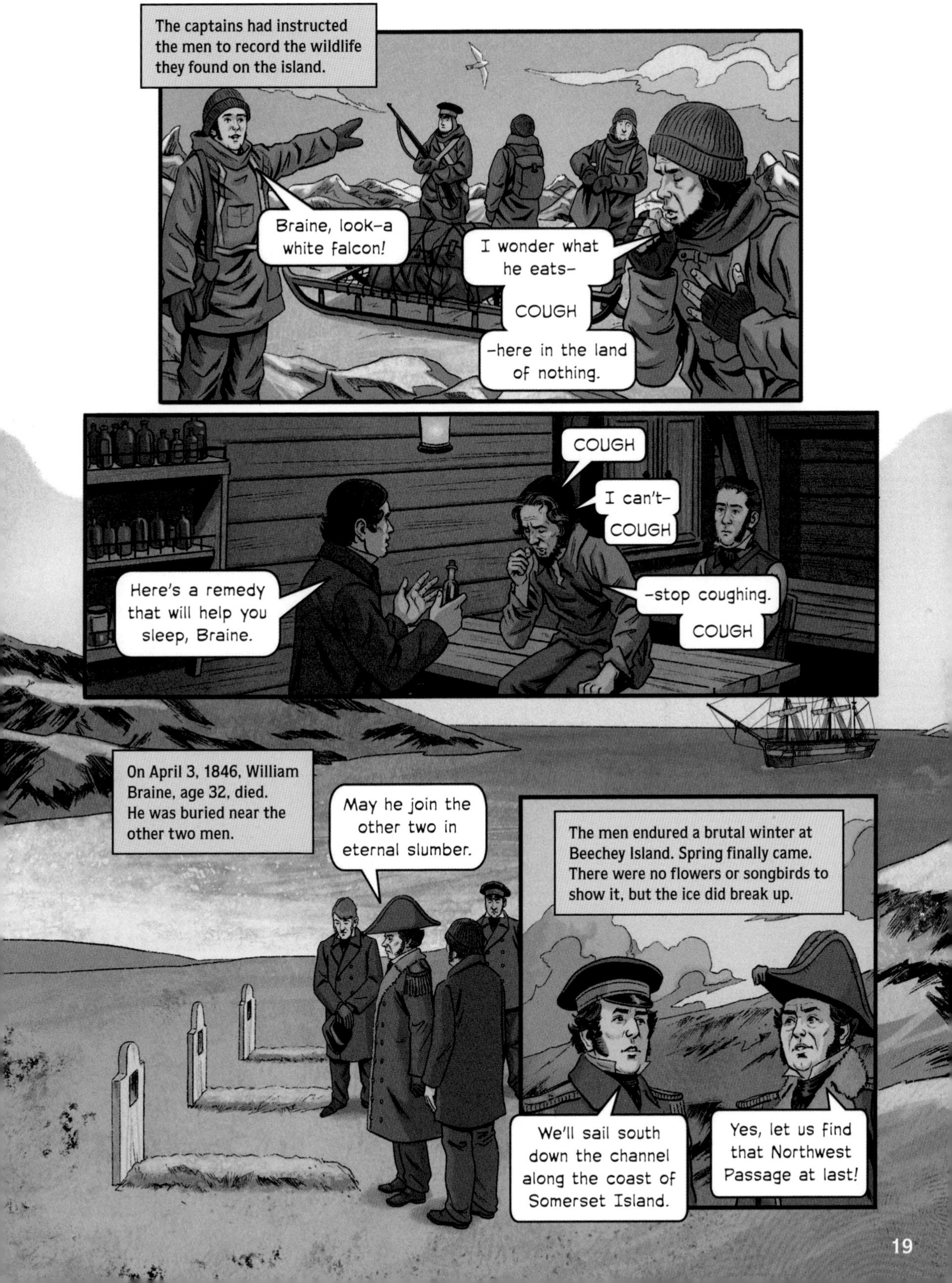
The captains had instructed the men to record the wildlife they found on the island.
Braine, look—a white falcon!
I wonder what he eats—
COUGH
—here in the land of nothing.
COUGH
I can't—
COUGH
Here's a remedy that will help you sleep, Braine.
—stop coughing.
COUGH
On April 3, 1846, William Braine, age 32, died. He was buried near the other two men.
May he join the other two in eternal slumber.
The men endured a brutal winter at Beechey Island. Spring finally came. There were no flowers or songbirds to show it, but the ice did break up.
We'll sail south down the channel along the coast of Somerset Island.
Yes, let us find that Northwest Passage at last!

Franklin's expedition spent the next four months slowly moving through 400 miles (644 km) of water choked with ice.

By September 12, 1846, the ships had made their way to the northernmost point of King William Island. But they once again found themselves trapped in the ice.

Have as many men as you can try to dig us out.

And if they can't?

We'll have to wait until spring again.

We're digging nowhere, Bailey! Just sweating!

We're keeping warm, Cann. Keep digging 'til the Captain tells us to stop.

Throughout the winter, the captains again had the men explore the area around the ships and on the island. They observed the wildlife and took notes on the weather, which could change drastically. In one day, it could be sunny, sleeting, snowing, and very windy.

Explorers built cairns, or stone landmarks, to mark their journeys. James Clark Ross had built one at Victory Point on King William Island during his Arctic expedition between 1829 and 1833.

A few men and I would like to see what we can find south of here.

Let me write a note for you to leave in Ross's cairn.

It was May 1847. The ice had shifted slightly, but the ships were still stuck. Lieutenant Gore and Mate Des Voeux had grown restless.

H.M.S. *Ships Erebus and Terror*
*wintered in the ice in*

*28 May 1847*     Lat *0 - 5 N*     Long *98 - 23 W*

*Having wintered in 1846–1847 at Beechey Island*
*after having ascended Wellington Channel*
*and returned by the West-side of Cornwallis Island*
*Sir John Franklin commanding the Expedition.*

*All Well*

Gore and Des Voeux led a group of men who took the note written by Captain Franklin and left it inside Ross's cairn. They continued south to chart unexplored territory.

What happened?

I was looking through field glasses.

When I brought them down, the cold metal ripped off my skin.

The men who stayed at the ships continued their own explorations and observations. The bitter cold continued to take its toll.

As May turned to June, the *Erebus* and the *Terror* remained stuck in the ice.

Then tragedy struck. On June 11, 1847, not two weeks after writing, "All well," Sir John Franklin died suddenly at the age of 61. Because no records have been found, it is unknown how he passed away.

Men, it is a somber time. But summer is upon us.

Let us hope for melting ice.

When will a search party be sent?

Not until next summer.

UGH, NO, none of us can take another year of this.

Days, weeks, and months passed, and the ice didn't melt. It kept the ships trapped and drifting south in its slow current. On top of that, men began to get sick in great numbers. No one knows for sure why. Current evidence suggests the men died of lead poisoning, a contagious lung disease called tuberculosis, and scurvy.

How many now?

Six officers and nine men. The sick bay is full too.

Save our souls . . .

By spring 1848, the ships had drifted to Cape Herschel on the south coast of the island.

Jumping Ship

By April 1848, the ships were still trapped. Nine officers and 15 men had died. With 105 men still alive, Captain Crozier decided to abandon the ships.

We'll follow the Back's Fish River to the fur-trading outpost.

Grab everything you can and load the sledges, men.

Do we tell them it's more than 700 miles away?

No. Did you see their faces when I said we were leaving? They had hope.

On April 22, 1848, the remaining officers and crew abandoned the ships.

The group walked 17 miles (27 km) across the ice to Ross's cairn at Victory Point. Captain Crozier and Captain Fitzjames updated the note they had left the year before.

*25th of April 1848 HMS Erebus & Terror were deserted on the 22nd of April 1848. Having been beset since the 12 September 1846. The officers and crew consisting of 105 souls. Sir John Franklin died on the 11th of June 1847 and the total loss of deaths in the expedition has been to this date 9 officers and 15 men.*

*Signed F.R.M Crozier, Captain and Senior Officer*

*Signed James Fitzjames, Captain HMS Erebus*

*and start tomorrow, 26th for Back's Fish River*

The next day, on April 26, 1848, the survivors started down the coast of King William Island. They never returned home.

Back in England, after not hearing from her husband for two years, Lady Franklin pushed to get search parties sent. The Royal Navy said the ships had enough food for three years. There was no need to worry until 1848. The first search party was sent in 1848. It returned in 1849, having not seen a trace of either ship.

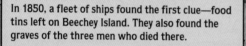

In 1850, a fleet of ships found the first clue—food tins left on Beechey Island. They also found the graves of the three men who died there.

Back in London that same year, Sir John Franklin and his crew were officially declared dead. But then a surveyor named Dr. John Rae returned to London with a new story. He said a group of Inuit people on King William Island had seen white men struggling to survive in the cold and snow.

In 1854, searchers built the Northumberland House on Beechey Island. They stocked it with food in case the Franklin expedition ever returned.

In April 1859, Lieutenant William Hobson found Ross's cairn and the Victory Point note inside. As of today, it is the only record of what happened to the *Erebus* and the *Terror*.

Between 1847 and 1880, more than 30 search parties tried to find out what happened to the *Erebus* and the *Terror*. The searchers found tin cans, snow goggles, and other objects used by the expedition.

More than 100 years later, in 2010 a final search for the lost expedition began. In 2014, with the help of Canada's national parks service, Parks Canada, and Inuit communities, the search party found the HMS *Erebus*. When the research ship made a detour through Terror Bay two years later, it discovered the HMS *Terror*. Both ships had sank.

# MAP OF THE EXPEDITION

## SIR JOHN FRANKLIN'S FINAL ARCTIC EXPEDITION

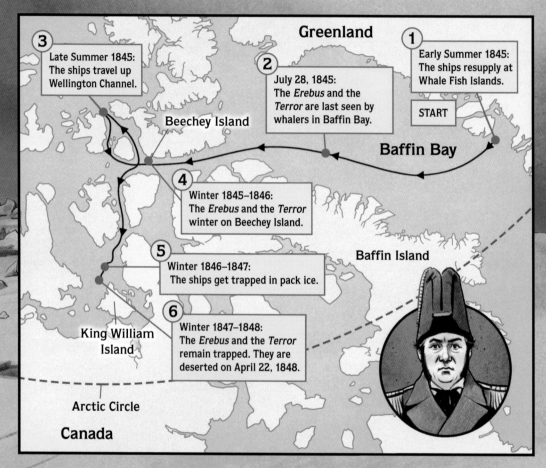

**Greenland**

**③** Late Summer 1845: The ships travel up Wellington Channel.

**②** July 28, 1845: The *Erebus* and the *Terror* are last seen by whalers in Baffin Bay.

**①** Early Summer 1845: The ships resupply at Whale Fish Islands.

START

Beechey Island

**Baffin Bay**

**④** Winter 1845–1846: The *Erebus* and the *Terror* winter on Beechey Island.

**⑤** Winter 1846–1847: The ships get trapped in pack ice.

**Baffin Island**

**⑥** Winter 1847–1848: The *Erebus* and the *Terror* remain trapped. They are deserted on April 22, 1848.

King William Island

Arctic Circle

**Canada**

So what happened to the crew? Two main theories remain. One is that the men returned to the ships. They managed to sail farther south before the two ships finally sank. Some survivors may have lived a few more years, according to Inuit sightings.

Another theory is that all the men died along the coast of King William Island. Inuits did see them in the area. Additionally, human remains have been found in 35 locations, thanks to Inuit and Euro-American search expeditions. It is unknown who the remains are of.

The Victory Point note on King William Island is the only written record of the expedition. But since the two ships were found in 2014 and 2016, perhaps more questions will be answered in the future about Sir Franklin and his quest to find the Northwest Passage.

# MORE ABOUT THE EXPEDITION

Thomas Morgan is the fourth grave on Beechey Island. He died a few years after the first three men during an expedition to find out what happened to the *Erebus* and the *Terror*.

In 1906, the Norwegian explorer Roald Amundsen finally found the Northwest Passage.

Dr. Owen Beattie began a project in 1981 to collect remains from King William Island. He wanted to identify the crew and their causes of death. He found a lot of lead in the bones he examined. He believed lead poisoning may have contributed to the deaths of the men.

Hartnell's body was dug up in 1984 and studied. Experts now believe he died from a lung infection combined with lead poisoning.

The darkest discovery about the expedition is that the last survivors ate their fallen friends in order to survive. Knife marks, broken bones, and heated bones gave scientists that evidence.

The HMS *Erebus* was found in 2014. The HMS *Terror* was found in 2016, 45 miles (72 km) away from the *Erebus*.

# GLOSSARY

**ascend** (uh-SEND)—to move up or in a northern direction

**cairn** (KAYRN)—a human-made pile of stones, sometimes used as a marker

**contagious** (kun-TAY-juss)—spreadable, as in a disease

**daguerreotype** (dag-EAR-oh-type)—an early photographic process in which an image is produced on a silver-coated copper plate

**gangrene** (GANG-green)—a condition that occurs when flesh decays, or rots

**infamous** (IN-fuh-muhss)—having an evil or detestable reputation

**lieutenant** (loo-TEN-uhnt)—a rank in the military above sergeant and below captain

**provisions** (proh-VIZH-uns)—supplies of food, drink, and equipment for a journey

**scurvy** (SCURV-ee)—a deadly disease caused by lack of vitamin C; scurvy produces swollen limbs, bleeding gums, and weakness

**sick bay** (SICK BAY)—an area on a ship where sick people are cared for

**sledge** (SLEJ)—a sled-like vehicle on runners used to pull loads or passengers over snow or ice

**surveyor** (suhr-VAY-uhr)—someone who measures areas of land for builders or mapmakers

# READ MORE

Barone, Rebecca E.F. *Race to the Bottom of the Earth: Surviving Antarctica.* New York: Henry Holt and Company, 2021.

Hyde, Natalie. *Search for the Northwest Passage.* New York: Crabtree Publishing Company, 2018.

Phillips, Katrina M. *The Disastrous Wrangel Island Expedition.* North Mankato, MN: Capstone, 2022.

# INTERNET SITES

*A Very Special Piece of Paper*
historymuseum.ca/blog/a-very-special-piece-of-paper/

*Northwest Passage*
kids.britannica.com/students/article/Northwest-Passage/442473

*Northwest Passage Facts for Kids*
kids.kiddle.co/Northwest_Passage

# INDEX

# AUTHOR BIO

Photo Copyright © Jillian Raye Photography

Lisa M. Bolt Simons has published more than 50 nonfiction children's books, as well as four middle grade "choose your path" novels and an adult history book. She's twice received an Honorable Mention for the McKnight Artist Fellowship for Writers in Children's Literature. She's also received a Minnesota State Arts Board Grant and other accolades for her writing. Lisa is a proud mom to her science- and math-minded twin daughter and son. Originally from Colorado, Lisa lives in southern Minnesota with her husband, who also loves to read.

# ILLUSTRATOR BIO

Eugene Smith was born in San Francisco, California, and spent his formative years in the small city of Pasadena, just outside of Los Angeles. Growing up in a suburb allowed Eugene to cultivate his imagination at a young age, and he began to read voraciously as well as illustrate the countless characters and stories that he conjured up in his mind. When he didn't spend his time drawing he consumed comic books, literature, and countless genre films that catapulted him into new and exciting worlds. Eugene studied painting and drawing at the Academy of Art University in San Francisco.